mmo
3251

# Two's Company

# 16 JAZZ DUETS
## for Two Clarinets

MUSIC MINUS ONE

Music Minus One

**mmo**

3251

# CONTENTS

ISBN 1-59615-739-9

# 1. A Swinger

# 2. A Study in Fragmentation

*8 beats (2 measures) precede music.*

# 3. For When Your Wife Gets Tired Of All That Jazz

*4 beats (1 measure) precede music.*

# 4. Back To Dixie

*8 beats (2 measures) precede music.*

# 5. Chinatown After Hours

*8 beats (2 measures) precede music.*

♩=184

# 6. For Lovers

*4 beats (1 measure) precede music.*

# 7. Mood With Variations

*1st clarinet:16 beats*
*(8 loud, 8 soft) precede music.*

*2nd clarinet:8 beats*
*(2 measures) precede music.*

# 8. Variations On A Fun Theme

# 9. Gypsy

*4 beats (1 measure) precede music.*

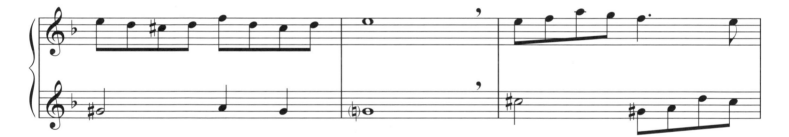

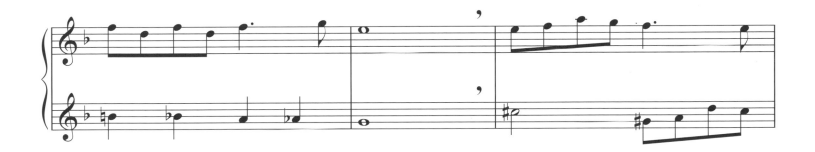

# 10. Harmonic / Rhythmic Study

*8 beats (2 measures) precede music.*

# 11. Riff Time

# 12. Blues, Ballad & Basie

*7 beats (1 ¾ measures) precede music.*

# 13. G Swing

*8 beats (2 measures) precede music.*

# 14. Just For Swinging

*8 beats (2 measures) precede music.*

# 15. Torchy

*8 beats (2 measures) precede music.*

Introduction

# 16. Triplet Study

*8 beats (2 measures) precede music.*

*Engraving: Wieslaw Novak*

MMO 3251

# JUST A SAMPLING OF ALBUMS FOR
# CLARINET
## FROM MUSIC MINUS ONE

## Pop, Blues & Jazz Classics

### Bluesaxe  Blues for Saxophone, trumpet or clarinet
MMO CD 4205

Bob Johnson, tenor saxophone - Eric Kriss, piano & electric piano; Bob Johnson, tenor and soprano sax; Stan Poplin, acoustic and electric bass; Jim Chanteloup, drums: Eight original blues compositions covering a broad range of styles from boogie-woogie to gospel to modern funk, for piano, bass, drums and sax. Listen, then play along. Complete arrangements for both E-flat and B-flat instruments.
*Tricky Dicky; When the Spirit; Cocaine Stomp; Wailer Blues; Boogie Breakdown; Tremblin'; Yacey's Fancy; Mad Dog Blues*

### Traditional Jazz Series  The Condon Gang  Adventures in New York & Chicago Jazz
MMO CD 3252

Bobby Gordon, clarinet - Hal Smith's Rhythmakers: Chris Tyle, trumpet; Clint Bakert, rombone; Anita Thomas, tenor saxophone; Ray Skjelbred, piano; Katie Cavera, guitar; Marty Eggers, bass; Hal Smith, drums: From the 1920s to the 1950s, Eddie Condon and his band created a unique style of traditional jazz, characterized by a succession of instrumental solos and abrupt transitions of dynamics; the result reverberates to this day in jazz. Now you can participate in this incredible style and the traditional music of the Condon Gang with this digital MMO release. A stellar lineup of professionals in a fabulous ensemble!
*I Know that You Know; Strut Miss Lizzie; Jazz Me Blues; Skeleton Jangle; Monday Date; The One I Love Belongs to Somebody Else; A Kiss to Build a Dream on; I Must Have that Man; Georgia Grind*

### Days of Wine & Roses  Sax Section Minus You
MMO CD 4210

Frank Wess, tenor sax - Bob Wilber All-Stars: Bob Wilber, soprano sax/clarinet; Hal McCusick, alto sax; Frank Wess, tenor sax/clarinet/flute; Joel Kaye, baritone sax & bass clarinet; Bernie Leighton, piano; George Duvivier, bass; Bill Goodwin, drums: Jazz legend Bob Wilber brings together a stylish set of classics scored for sax quartet, piano and rhythm section. The four-part voicing, a departure from the traditional big-band era five-man section, makes each voice all the more important and will enhance your pleasure in performing the missing part. Clarinetists will find all soprano parts easily playable; Tenor players can play the soprano parts directly with the added bonus of a chance to study the superb soloing of Frank Wess.
*Moon Mist; Days of Wine and Roses; Acapulco Princess; Two Moods for Piano and Winds; The Mighty Hudson; Early Morning Blues*

### Easy Jazz Duets - Two Clarinets and Rhythm Section
MMO CD 3213

The Benny Goodman Rhythm Section: George Duvivier, bass; Bobby Donaldson, drums: A delightful collection of easy-to-medium duets featuring you plus an all-star fellow instrumentalist, clarinetist Kenny Davern and rhythm section. 1st to 4th year.
*The Green Danube; Tone Colors; Reaching Up; Uptown-Downtown; Main Street; Ski Slope; Doing Your Chores; Stop and Go; Glider; Jumper; Da Dit; Hot Fudge; Tijuana; La De Da De; Switcheroo; Swing Easy; Hop Scotch; Swingin' in the Rain; 4/4 Waltz; One Note Break; Lazy; Bits and Pieces*

### For Saxes Only  tenor sax, trumpet or clarinet
MMO CD 4204

Bob Wilber, tenor sax; Hilton Jefferson, alto sax - The Bob Wilber All-Stars: Bob Wilber, tenor sax; Hilton Jefferson, alto sax; Jerome Richardson, alto sax; Seldon Powell, tenor sax; Danny Bank, baritone sax; Dick Wellstood, piano; George Duvivier, bass; Panama Francis, drums: Designed to give the jazz saxophonist (or clarinet or trumpet player) an opportunity to play with a top-flight sax section. Due to the comparative scarcity of big bands today, this is the one area in which young players sorely lack experience. The problems of sight-reading, intonation, phrasing, vibrato, unisons, subtone, etc. which the player will encounter in working with this album are the same one would face playing with Ellington, Basie or Goodman. If you haven't had the opportunity to work in a big band, playing with this album should give you an idea of that special thrill one gets when the blend is perfect and everybody's swinging together!
*Countdown; Might as Well Be Movin' On; Waltzing on a Reed; Ballad for Beth; Freemanition; Living for Love; Pork 'n' Beans; Blues for a Matador*

### From Dixie to Swing
MMO CD 3234

Kenny Davern, clarinet - Kenny Davern, clarinet & soprano sax; 'Doc' Cheatham, trumpet; Vic Dickenson, trombone; Dick Wellstood, piano; George Duvivier, bass; Gus JohnsonJr., drums: These Jazz legends back you up in this collection of 1950s 'Dixieland' standards performed in New York clubs such as Eddie Condon's and Nicks.. We encourage you as soloist to invent counter-melodies rather than mere harmony. This is a music of loose weaving parts, not one of precision ensemble figures. A great improvisational experience.
*Way Down Yonder in New Orleans; Red Sails in the Sunset; Second Hand Rose; Rose of Washington Square; On the Sunny Side of the Street; Exactly Like You; I Want a Little Girl; The Royal Garden Blues*

### In a League of His Own  *Pop Standards played by Ron Odrich and You*
MMO CD 3215

Ron Odrich, clarinet - The Al Raymond Orchestra; Mark Stallings, string synthesist: Join Ron in these pop classics. You won't be disappointed!
*All or Nothing at All; Come Rain or Come Shine; Stardust; The Coffee Song; Days of Wine and Roses; Emily; I Hadn't Anyone 'Til You; I Concentrate on You; If I Should Lose You; It Might as Well Be Spring; Saturday Night (Is the Loneliest Night of the Week)*

### Isle of Orleans
MMO CD 3253

Tim Laughlin, clarinet - Tim Laughlin's New Orleans All-Stars: Native son Tim Laughlin decided he wanted to create in the style, but not necessarily using the tried and true classics, of the "Crescent City." So he assembled an extraordinary band of players, all veterans of the music, wrote a collection of new songs, and produced this extraordinary album. It won First Prize as the Best Jazz Album created in Louisiana in 2003 by Offbeat Magazine. Tim graciously made this album available to Music Minus One, remixing the music to omit the key players, clarinet, trumpet, trombone, piano, bass and drums for some of the most delectable play-alongs we offer in our catalogue. This music is rich in tradition but new to your ears. This music isn't easy but then again, to modern players, it may be, as they'll be able to negotiate the charts provided. We've provide audio samples of each song. This is music for the ages, guaranteed to pleasure players from ten to ninety. The personnel of this band is extraordinary as you can see, and the music they make together has to be experienced. Listen, can you hear that band? **(2CD Set)**
*Magnolia Dance; Restless Heart; Blues for Faz; Suburban St. Parade; It's My Love Song to You; Gentilly Strut; I Know I'll See You Again; Crescent City Moon; Isle of Orleans; Monkey Hill*

### Jazz Standards with Rhythm Section
MMO CD 3218

Larry Linkin, clarinet - : Jazz standards with Larry Linkin as soloist guiding you. Then try them yourself with the rhythm section! **(2CD Set)**
*Sweet Georgia Brown; Memories of You; Claire de Lune/Moon River; Oh, Lady Be Good; Porgy and Bess: Summertime; Back Home Again in Indiana; Goodbye; One Note Samba; It Had To Be You; Autumn Leaves; Wolverine Blues; Amazing Grace; Here's that Rainy Day*

### Jazz Standards with Strings
MMO CD 3219

Larry Linkin, clarinet - : Superb jazz standards with string accompaniments; work your own artistry with this great ensemble! **(2CD Set)**
*When Sunny Gets Blue; What'll I Do; That's All; I've Got It Bad and That Ain't Good; In a Sentimental Mood; Our Love Is Here to Stay; Embraceable You; What Are You Doing the Rest of Your Life?; 'Tis Autumn; Night and Day; But Beautiful; Darn That Dream; Ain't Misbehavin'; When I Fall in Love*

### Lee Konitz Sax Duets
MMO CD 4110

Lee Konitz, saxophone - Lee Konitz and the MMO orchestra/various: Jam with the legendary Lee Konitz on this power-packed album of sax duets. Includes straight duets as well as duets with rhythm section and orchestral backgrounds! Features a wide range of music, from New Orleans to standards to Bossa Nova. Contains both E-flat and B-flat parts, and can be used by alto or tenor sax players, as well as clarinetists and trumpeters. You simply will not want to miss this album, one of the most requested classic titles from the vast MMO catalogue.
*You Go to My Head; Meditation; Three Little Words; Somewhere; Blues in A-flat; Waltz; Free Form No. 1; Free Form Ballad; Basin Street Blues*

### Play Lead in a Sax Section
MMO CD 4209

Hal McKusick, solo alto saxophone - Bob Wilber All-Stars: Bob Wilber, soprano sax/clarinet; Frank Wess, tenor sax/clarinet/flute; Joel Kaye, baritone sax & bass clarinet; Bernie Leighton, piano; George Duvivier, bass; Bill Goodwin, drums: Sequel to 'For Saxes Only' offers a series of saxophone quartets (rather than the typical 5-piece arrangement from the big-band era). Hal McKusick provides a complete version to use samples for the improvisational sections, and you have the option of playing the notated solo, or improvising your own.
*The Look of Love; All Too Soon; No More Blues; Century Plaza; In an Old Deserted Ballroom; A Little Farewell Music*

### Ron Odrich Plays Standards plus You
MMO CD 3220

Ron Odrich, clarinet - (rhythm section: A broad-based album of popular standards; listen to this master perform, then try it yourself with the rhythm section.
*April in Paris; Oh My Head; Embraceable You; Porgy and Bess: The Man I Love; Body and Soul; Poor Butterfly; What Is This Thing Called Love?; Lover Come Back to Me; I Only Have Eyes for You; Sometimes I'm Happy*

### Sinatra Set to Music  *Kern, Weill, Gershwin, Howard and You*
MMO CD 3216

Ron Odrich, clarinet - The Al Raymond Orchestra: Ron Odrich plays these great Sinatra standards, then you take center stage the second time around! Great pieces for improving your musicianship.
*Steppin' Out with My Baby; That's All; Angel Eyes; It Was a Very Good Year; Embraceable You; Body and Soul; Fly Me to the Moon; Yesterdays; Prisoner of Love; Here's that Rainy Day; Speak Low*

### Southern Winds: Jazz Flute Jam
MMO CD 3376

Maurice Gainen, flute - The Maurice Gainen Band: Jazz master Maurice Gainen has assembled a stellar assortment of jazz standards with a quality all their own. Listen to Mr. Gainen's interpretations, then you join the ensemble as the star player! Includes C, B-flat and E-flat parts and is perfectly suited to virtually any instrument!
*Little Linda; Black Orpheus; Blue Bossa; Meditation; Just Friends; Samba de Orfeo; Feel Like Makin' Love; Comin' Home Baby; Mercy, Mercy, Mercy*

### Stompin' & Struttin' the New Swing  *Six Bands on a Hot Tin Roof*  MMO CD 3237

Around 1998, a new swing sound came to our music. Derived in part from the Big Bands of the Forties, and tempered by the music of such jump bands as Louis Prima and Louis Jordan, besides adopting the dress code of the hip-cats of an earlier era (Cab Calloway for instance) these bands played some great music in a more modern, flexible and fun-drenched style. We've taken the most famous songs of these groups, and put them all on an MMO CD for your pleasure and participation.
*Hey, Pachuco; The Indigo Swing (style of Indigo Swing); Zip Gun Bop (style of The Royal Crown Review); Put a Lid on It (style of The Squirrel Nut Zippers); Hell (style of The Squirrel Nut Zippers); You and Me and the Bottle Makes Three Tonight (Baby) (style of Big Bad Voodoo Daddy); Zoot Suit Riot (style of The Cherry Poppin' Daddies); Jump, Jive & Wail (style of The Brian Setzer Orchestra); This Cat's on a Hot Tin Roof (style of The Brian Setzer Orchestra)*

### Traditional Jazz Series:  Chicago-Style Jam Session
MMO CD 3239

Evan Christopher, clarinet - Jon-Erik Kellso, trumpet; Mike Pittsley, trombone; Brian Ogilvie, tenor saxophone; Jeff Barnhart, piano; Bill Huntington, guitar; Jim Singleton, bass; Hal Smith, drums: This exciting 2-CD set emphasizes collectively improvised ensembles and the succession of individual solos in the freewheeling "Chicago-Style" offshoot of New Orleans Jazz. The rhythmic texture is rooted in the swing feel of the late 1930s, and the instrumentation is typical of the New York groups of this genre. The songs are popular melodies from the 1900s to 1930s as well as multithematic compositions and blues—you'll find such classics as "'Deed I Do," "Sugar," "The Darktown Strutters' Ball," "That's a Plenty" and more. Chicago-style jazz is named for the city where it first developed. In the 1920s, many New Orleans musicians, including "Jelly Roll" Morton, Louis Armstrong, the Original Dixieland Jazz Band, and the New Orleans Rhythm Kings actively performed and recorded in Chicago. Many younger musicians were profoundly influenced by their music, including Eddie Condon, Benny Goodman, Gene Krupa, Muggsy Spanier and many others. By the 1930s many of these same musicians moved on to New York. As the Big Band era closed, improvising soloists still found work in New York clubs such as Nick's, Condon's and the Metropole. The texture was distinctly in the New Orleans tradition but the language was Swing and directly reflected the synthesis that took place in Chicago. This stylistically accurate recording demonstrates the inner workings of collective improvisation in a traditional jazz context. You'll be blown away by the quality of this jazz combo. Includes both printed solo part and a concert lead sheet, to give you a rare glimpse into the workings of the bands of the times. **(2CD Set)**
*The Darktown Strutters' Ball; That's A Plenty; Rosetta; Poor Butterfly; Sugar (That Sugar Baby o'Mine); 'Deed I Do; Blues (My Naughty Sweetie Gives to Me); The Royal Garden Blues*

### Visions  The Clarinet Artistry of Ron Odrich
MMO CD 3214

Ron Odrich, clarinet - Lew Soloff, trumpet/flugelhorn; David Fink, bass; David Ratajczak, drums; John Basili, guitar Sammy Figueroa, percussion; Marc Copeland, piano; John Corbert, synthesizer/Larry Fallon (Arranger): Match skills with one of the finest clarinetists in jazz with original material and standards, ballads and Latin stylings, plus an exquisite classical selection. Both the listening and the playing are exceedingly exciting and worthwhile. For intermediate-to-advanced players. Enjoy! **(2CD Set)**
*I Love You Just the Way You Are; Two for the Road; El Cajon; Concerto in C minor: II. Adagio; Only Trust Your Heart; Daphne's Vision; Highway Vision; Visions of Nina Marie; A Vision of the Hamptons; It Might as Well Be Spring; Street of Dreams; My Foolish Heart*

### When Jazz Was Young
MMO CD 3829

Bob Wilber All Stars: Bob Wilber, clarinet; Buck Clayton, trumpet; Vic Dickenson, trombone; Bud Freeman, tenor sax; Dick Wellstood, piano; Abdul Malik, bass; Panama Francis, drums: One look at the player's list on this album will reveal some of the most famous veterans of the jazz era ('30s through '60s). An opportunity to jam with these jazz giants should not be missed. Under the leadership of Bob Wilber (he scored the film 'Cotton Club'), they present a memorable hour of music-making you'll not soon forget!
*Keepin' out of Mischief Now; Chimes Blues; A Star Is Born: The Man that Got Away; Do You Know What it Means to Miss New Orleans; Tin Roof Blues; Wild Man Blues; Milenberg Joys; Wolverine Blues; When the Saints Go Marchin' in (arr. Bob Wilber); Basin Street Blues*

---

**For our full catalogue of clarinet releases, including more popular and jazz titles, classical concerti, chamber works and master classes**
**visit us on the web at**

# www.musicminusone.com

Call 1-800 669-7464 in the USA • 914 592-1188 International • Fax: 914 592-2751
50 Executive Blvd. • Elmsford, NY 10523
email: mmogroup@musicminusone.com